salmonpoetry

Favorite Bedtime Stories

John M. Fitzgerald

Published in 2014 by
Salmon Poetry
Cliffs of Moher, County Clare, Ireland
Website: www.salmonpoetry.com
Email: info@salmonpoetry.com

ISBN 978-1-908836-70-0

COVER IMAGE: Alexandra Eldridge – *How I Have Lived Inside of Books.*
COVER DESIGN & TYPESETTING: *Siobhán Hutson*
Printed in Ireland by Sprint Print

Foreword

by Rex Wilder

I want to be John Fitzgerald's baby. Well, his wife's anyway. If he has one; I'm not so sure sorcerers are in the habit of mating for life or raising children anywhere but several inches off the ground. And safe alone with Fitzgerald as a boy barely three feet tall and years old? Not with his imagination and penchant for naughtiness. I imagine myself propped up breathless in the bottom bunk at seven each evening, a gold dusk dusting my fresh features from the window over whose generous glass Dad would refuse to draw the blinds, fuzzy blanket pulled up to my neck, ice water clinking beside me, when my idol would make his Grand Entrance, an imaginary book of fairy tales in his right hand and the promise of my unconsciousness in his left. Or subconsciousness, I should say. Because Fitzgerald is a master at entering without knocking, weaving a spell and leaving it like a quilt as his calling card, both to keep one warm and to wonder where he went. Another sly poet, the great and under-appreciated William Meredith, could have been writing this introduction when he wrote in his "Sonnet on Rare Animals," "Startled or on a signal, what is rare/ Is off before you have it anywhere." At the same time, I could advise the reader of this rewarding collection to heed the advice of Meredith's friend Robert Frost, who reminds us that "Heaven gives its glimpses only to those/ Not in a position to look too close." So look away if you can. Close your eyes. Ask your attorney or talking dog to read these poems aloud to you, and be prepared to fall under their spell. Later on you can study the lines, their craft and craftiness. Because nothing's by accident in Fitzgerald and it's only human to want to know how the magician did it. Although if the poet has his way you will be anything but human in the throes of his transportation. As he advises us, "The world fears a human being/ and when we catch one// We tie it to strings/ and drag it behind cars at weddings/ for the musical sparks left in its wake." !

Contents

At Least Eighteen New Poems

Acknowledgments

All right, we have a lot to get through so let's get started.
A shout out to the following for their support
of these poems and this book:
The Warwick Review
The Passionate Transitory
The Toronto Quarterly
MadHat Review
Levure Littéraire
Tiferet Journal
December
The Original Van Gogh's Ear Anthology
Life and Legends
Love's Peripetiass
Asian Signature

A significant percentage of the individual lines in
The Charter of Effects debuted
as my *Facebook* statuses over the course of several years.
Alexandra Eldridge did the cover art:
How I Have Lived Inside of Books.
Hélène Cardona, well, twelve years we've been inseparable,
joined at the hip, many say.

In memory of my father, John J. FitzGerald,
who died at 42 of the unpronounceable.
He never recited any of these, like I did to my poor sons.

This is a puzzle, let's put it together.

Epigram

From Herotoclus, the Uncouth:

"You fucking people come here expecting poetry?"

Note the Ancient Islandic translates more literally:

"you children of goats come here expecting poetry?"

He was scheduled to read outside the library on the island
the very moment of the famous utterance.

In all fairness Herotoclus was, at the time,
the only one facing the tidal wave.

One can see though how he deserves his moniker.

So I've been working on these *Title-At-The-Bottom* pieces
and up to now have only two.
You know at every reading there's this moment
when the poet steps up to the mic
and begins to break the ice with jokes,
or thanks those who made it possible,
or other readers, or all of you for coming out,
and sometimes, like now, if you're lucky,
the so-called poem will have started
before you noticed and is over. Painless. Okay.

Enough Fooling Around

By the way,
that's the title at the bottom:
"enough fooling around"
is written in here,
and so is what I'm saying to you now.

The Next Poem Is

The Man Who Knew Everything

Sapiens number seven billion.
And it's the same with me as with every other human.
I formed immersed in a dark sac of fluid
and bore through a tunnel into the light.

From that time I have never been alone.
From that time too I have always been.
I am a hypothetical being.
Every person born of my line

the day and year and place that I was,
and given my features, strengths, and limitations,
would almost certainly be me.
For over a year did I write certain nights when I could.

Orator for the planet with a voice like dirt
and a few odd ghosts behind me.
Herein lies the testament of earth,
a statement much too much for me to bear.

It overwhelms me, and I am afraid.
I have no proof.
I am poet and cannot explain.
I will go into the other room to drink.

My God, my love is way out of control.
All manner of loneliness I pray to.
I will be like the far thoughts of paper.
When the word existed before it was spoken.

Fairy Tale

Once, there were four brothers.
One owned all the water.
One owned all the fire,
one owned all the food,
and one owned all the air.
We stuffed these leeches in a hole
and ate and drank and breathed.

The Becoming

That which is above is from that which is below, and that which is below is from that which is above, working the miracles of one.

– Hermes Trismegistus

I have become one of these humans.
From beyond I return in the literal way,
with account of both the transit and its feeling.

Thought recedes like a land bridge covered with sea
in the days when the flood struck awe in every heart
to set me once again among you – it has been so long.

I come down from above your lights,
on a redeye over metropolises, aglow with electricity,
from Atlanta to far stretching City of Angels.

I come down, backward in time,
across shades of altitude and night,
it has been so long.

Atlanteans, Angelinos, I pod unto thee, over waves
and basic cables, fiber optically, eye-glassed and fire worked.
It has been so very long.

I reappear thrice great to now,
philosopher over all earth's meanings,
an architect mistook in scripture,

a little one, already ancient, with cracks for veins.
To the latent, pagan icons,
to the Latin, and classical Greek, it has been so long.

To the offspring of Ardi and Lucy and Ötzi,
to the Jutes and the Saxons and Celts, it has been so long.
Humans! Time to move. We are of another age, revising.

Reliers on dogma, so long. Borders all over the globe, so long,
for I am lover of the word since the beginning,
and that earth seems to move I believe.

It is a fool who grows a crop then does not harvest,
for he is left with a crop of insects.
The thoughts of the mind are a crop.

Take these in and realize.
So long, disconnected descendants.
Misleaders and users, so long.

You knew, or should have known,
what gets scratched by flesh into stone.
Thus I am born among Sapiens, to exact humanity.

You swear, when you hear, I am coiner of words,
my poem a garment, painted rosily. Sing to it. Erect it at the fair.
Impress whatever tiny spark in you may listen.

114 million years ago the first flower spat
its never seen color out of earth.
A flower heretofore latent in humans is about to burst.

Spread the word, now understanding is at hand.
The new human, with a book 13 billion years in the making.
God, it has been so long.

Should we just rest a moment?
My work is done here, really.
Though I did come up with a third
title at the bottom poem.
I should've told you before now.
I have no choice but notice what I do.
Observations give me thoughts like these.
And every word I read is written down.
Of course!
How else could I read it if it wasn't written down?

This Isn't Magic

Devolution

Ceaselessly flick me with light.
I buzz 'round in circles a one-winged fly,
will waylaid by sheer brute strength,
free to believe as I'm told or be beaten.

I remember all this when I hear the alarm,
and I'm so hung over yet have to wake.
I cannot stand that race again
but I am the meat to be eaten this day.

Alert, I take to trees
where serpents sing children lullabies.
Mothers decode their forbidden language:
Hush, the snake is on the prowl.

I stake out my limb and begin to nod
when my strings get jerked with that fear of falling.
A reflex from leftover monkeys, crushed,
at the end of a dream about flying away.

The Ape's Notion

Opposing conditions, which may or may not be earthen,
angels of rain, fairies of twilight, forces of wind,
desiring sweets, grasses, and root,
give me the sum of all prayer till I want nothing further.

Open profounder, intimate spaces.
Still existence. Beckon forth.
For there are days that none can find me,
and the stream runs down the mountain to the ocean.

Who don't believe in the animals?
Frog-step. We're twisting hip.
Blown on like a wish.
Time is my address now.

Let the child-ape come 'round,
that I might ask what it remembers
of the emptiness it came from.
Do our same gods play different games?

Weren't we animals, would we be cold?
Sleep in the trees so as not to be eaten.
Think of everyone as a feast, everyone.
Lion one day dragged in pieces by the ants before their queen.

Thus I worship fruit and branch
from behind eyes where the wood creaks and the leaf sways.
For I am ape, having in me ape blood,
and am loved better by The Tree than any animal.

Leopard

The strut says I am, ooh, much more physical than you.
I've crouched on a limb and considered giraffe.
You'd *better* climb.
I'll be up that tree on your primate ass.

Where I am men hide.
I'll slap you like the monkey you are.
Paws out, already back, slapped again from the other side.
Two three times 'til you know you've been hit.

I like the instant you cling to the claw before you flop.
You think in that moment you might get away.
I love your hope.
It makes me growl.

I'll let you get a little in before I pounce.
Oblong, imbalanced. Bet your feet slide out,
smart guy, language-man, who's serious now?
Brain, meet mister tooth.

Lullyby

(for Chris)

I shall now sing you a lullyby.
It goes a little something like this:

Ahem, mi, mi, mi…

Burglars come
at night, when you are sleeping
and if you're still awake
they chop your stinking head off
so go to bed now
and get yourself some rest

Wasn't that a lovely lullyby?
Would you like to hear the second verse?

Tooth Fairies

They come, or cross over, in measured degree
proportionately as I ignore them
to provide for orderly creation

Make any point possess the whole
and understand the secret
of the teardrop that I came from

Allow the smoke to dissipate
the reek to wane, or rearrange
as I was saying

All I really need
has been revealed to me in fairy tales
They fashion piano keys from our teeth

to produce that twinkling sound in flight
It's a thriving trade, so they have charts
much as butchers do for meat

Canine, molar, bicuspid
each fetches its particular price
But as I said, they enter in

and run around through holes in my head
like bugs weighing my mind
beneath my pillow as I dream

They leave as payment
the equivalent of my aspirations
which is always a quarter

They come only at night
because all the world fears a human being
and when we catch one

we tie it to strings
and drag it behind cars at weddings
for the musical sparks left in its wake

The Charter of Effects

Parts I - XV

"And those who were seen dancing were thought to be insane by those who could not hear the music."

FRIEDRICH NIETZSCHE

Dramatis Personae

Counsel is a lawyer driven by money.

The Likeness of the Universe is a poet addicted
to life-changing lines.

The Idol is whatever gets in the way, here taken
by mouth as needed.

A *commentator* analyzes.

Various Muses, including *Summer*, *Orpheus*, *Presence*,
Polyhymnia, *Faith*, *Xena*, and *Hope*, appear at their leisure,

with cameos by *O'Hara*, *Rilke*, *Crane*, and *Berryman.*

I.

First, the muses.
Any fool could see he was infested with infinite muses.
Mere mention makes writers like me unsure.
But having now done so unlocks a secret

I'm not so certain I want to reveal
so much as render a logical explanation.
This is how the Likeness became infected.
Ghost picked raw by muses, themselves in decay.

Counsel tried alcohol, myriad ruses,
attempted with smoke to coax them away,
hammered the tuner till stars spun about,
mixed himself up with a spoon and a rope.

Strewn feelings might settle for certain ambitions,
leaving restlessness to anticipate.
Perhaps even more so than anything else,
feeling should be described before it tries to go outside itself.

There must be evidence of pain.
The truth *for now* a lie on which its future can be based.
Our backs together, unturned
on a sphere we stand distanced as possible.

Muses in mind, Counsel cares, in abeyance,
until later when memory no longer relates.
Entire illusions of innerness pray if only rain were beer.
Should instead he hear her coming she is lovely, but he doesn't.

Counsel plots against muses however it seems.
Let him never rush headlong to any emotion.
Everyone every day, little has changed.
Periods of waiting tolled.

An act, to reconcile. See?
Who was in charge of tequila?
Miscellaneous provisions, findings and purposes, come out.
We've sacrificed ourselves again.

II.

Muses hover everywhere, to see through.
To jump from the monotonous lingering
of essentially an edge, transformed by point of view
into an artist's rendering of someone missing.

So contends the Likeness of the universe.
Fateful muses gone to curse, he's had your number.
All we need now is a charm, or delusion –
a general denial that any of us really hurts.

What if glyphs replace the music in his head.
A weeping one can hardly stand, who would it serve?
Muses cut in, without room, like a cab,
as if you owe them some salvation.

They often light exquisite as a lung awaits a breath.
He says hold them in for as long as you can,
suck out their sockets till every revenant is dead,
make them rue the day they became a man.

Counsel loves pointing in every direction,
will spring a dealer or a killer,
mean whatever you expected,
hock your mother's house for payment.

He'll eventually bury the Likeness of light
in a box he made of air for dreaming.
Evaporate, you stardust!
The bars are awaiting the stakes to be raised.

Abandon queues, get out while the piano's playing.
Set it aside for sake of delay, give nothing.
You're talking to one now, man,
with an edge on his line too concise to repeal.

Peridotic olivine things blink.
And not just reflections, but eyes that smolder.
They rearrange, and man, he don't care like I do.
In advance, the exchange, or stay where you are.

III.

Little hand three, big nine finds the Likeness
indestructible, interpreting a slur, a hum too.
He'll hire a cartoonist for his thoughts.
Counsel moved twice for a loophole – 'twas denied.

Loosen up, exhibit signs.
Life is in the fire, somewhere.
Seal the cracks where it tries getting through.
That can't just mean prophets talking to the stupid.

Phoenicians brought me ABCs.
You *should* be afraid, I write and drive,
can't look in any direction without reading something.
A regalia of car horns announces my arrival

so do not move off your footprints till I leave.
Hanging a left, eyes flicker the mix.
I sense hesitation yet defer
not so much to the cliff, but the bottom.

Where once we dreamt of paradise,
between the rivers, shock and awe.
In the empire of a thousand crimes per martyr
lies the water for which all humans are willing to trade.

No more than a gulp, or swallow.
The Likeness fading in and out
with a chance of spinning, or blurring.
Nearby mere sun unplucks the string

at a place where drops converge replete
with microscopic teeming,
elements distill into a discontented reveille.
The weed pried through the highway cracks imbibed.

Gilgamesh cried over Enkidu.
The people of Uruk diverted Euphrates
to bury their king in the riverbed.
How the Likeness weeps too at his own incantations.

IV.

Counsel writes on the road, in chalk,
for convenience, leaning either way.
Says the brilliance of the Likeness is he's weak, afraid,
he pines while I forget your name.

He don't let cell phones interrupt
and articulates what I disclaim.
I swat the muses off me when he leaves.
Watch them ascend to my decrease.

No motion's ever argued free.
That poet enrages at my enlargement.
The Likeness can't even breathe but smoke.
He knew me before, when I sold him a nickel.

Names for the muses, how could it hurt?
He fascinates with puzzles like insane,
says not a word more than needed,
and swigs down his escape.

Counsel can wipe that look off your face.
Swipe a password before you have time to erase.
Yeah, he is quick, he'll nail you,
will tell you how many make five.

He drafts *documents*, you know,
straight from his own, ridiculous sense of fairness,
of which there is little likelihood of appearance,
every muse another calculated risk.

The Likeness redoubles his doubt every day.
Doesn't think of anything he can't.
Unscrewed from his addictions, then what?
Picture yourself remembering lines.

The Likeness gathered us here to reflect.
Confused on the surface, the depths concur.
Between boggling, irrelevant arguments, slip in reason.
Every so often, one sticks, I'm sure.

V.

Three shots into emptiness, despairing.
Hell is awake when the liquor store's closed
and the spirits all are drunk.
The row to excellence concise, need I say less?

Counsel renounces rhyme's every invention.
He's after a third to apply toward a Jag.
Such a twister of systems grown iPod dependent,
deleted you in his mind but then refrained,

just like he didn't run you over on your bike.
There is an answer. You either have it or you don't.
No normal poet would put up with this.
The Likeness almost forgets himself.

Counsel once found semblance at the nether end of teeter totter,
exactly in the spot he left it –
feet dangling content and knees bent in regret.
Nepenthean, the word sought, how perfect could it get?

From that speedily exhausted smudge of memory,
all its profanities anchored in place
by scorpioid reasonings in the shadow of a meteor,
picture first, then word erased,

to the promises of music makers ringing,
mired in diminished mythology,
deign to sigh,
pretend to elevate each other just to let the lever fly.

It's great when invocation works.
Every local god is summoned.
But while they piece last night together,
let's work on further fragmenting today.

As much he rains, and no further, like Sanskrit.
Boneless, approaching the bottleneck,
a hole enrapt with each inflection glides.
For *this* bloody muses cut into my line.

VI.

Everybody looks disgusted.
Her image drives me to the breeze.
Plays tricks on a teardrop, to compensate,
as if some very deep scar affects conviction.

The Likeness taught the muses what they mean.
They didn't make him poet.
A molecule could muse, for all it's worth.
What is it fireflies glow about?

Recall the ever lovely Summer,
junkie of the mind, gone off on her spell to relate:
Incite me. I'll portion up your lot in life.
Agitate the mighty clay, and blow the dust about to spite me.

To attribute with purity doesn't seem right.
What of her dangerous wit can I conceive?
I'll flay the beams to their never known knees,
and just barely get by an equation.

So what next? An understanding?
I don't think so, at least not yet.
Feelings look different among themselves.
It would be sheer luck if two were the same.

Hunger's as close to pain as a burn,
or as fear is to manifestation.
And feelings like loneliness zoned to hurt,
seem like, in fact, no more than breaking.

I float like a streak into mirth.
Row three hundred miles into ocean
to verify ancestral darkness, where sure enough stars exist
amid Great Rifts and Coalsack nebulae.

Darkness and cold is the natural state.
Enough to petrify a flame.
I am diviner, look in my eyes at the next best thing to light.
Background black, specks silent.

VII.

It doesn't throb, the earth is turning.
The Likeness predicted it would.
Thought he was wrong when he was right – his first mistake.
The idol hurts to do its work.

Counsel evolves in isolation.
He pleads, he moves, reiterates,
gets worked up just talking to himself.
The Likeness says quit your bitchin'.

Would still convert a bank to a café.
Hypocrite! Make sure all you want is to be alone.
You're angrier at yourself for fearing to break the law
than for pretending to have principles.

Counsel pisses the Likeness off.
A general fanfare follows everywhere he goes.
He stresses each embalming syllable.
Has a consuming dissatisfaction this makes up for.

He could be condescending but thinks few would understand.
Is more like pain than anything that is not pain.
I rest my forehead in my hands,
take comfort in their seeming to belong.

To be *alone*?
Do you even know where the Tylenol is?
You're like a lobster seller at McDonald's.
And this, the first few minutes awake.

Mirror, you'd better do a better job of faking.
A hand just slid across your throat but decided not to shave.
Who knows what that means?
How much does your head weigh?

Oh man, little Orpheus tearing it up.
At least five layers of tongue erased.
Everyone trusts me more than I do.
Counsel has a Likeness to displace.

VIII.

Somehow, became the Likeness
designated monitor to one poetic evolution,
referred to, increasingly, as sort of a yearning.
And this is not just muses' doings.

The Likeness would stone himself for a structure.
Is multiplied into composite numbers
faster than factored back into his prime.
A hologram with its entire rage inside it.

He trained his children not to kill him.
Is thirty years it at tag for lack of effort.
Was happier when he still believed in magic.
In self-fulfilling phases, fades the Likeness.

Muses jump from mind to mind,
black holes swallow galaxies, the universe itself a tie.
If only he knew everything.
A Zoroastrian, pansophic Spock.

He could write then.
Prefer his own thoughts to your voice.
Muses draw the music out,
fingerprint an afternoon. Euphonic!

Deeper feelings fear the light,
which lets them finally see they bleed.
They bled in dark too, just hadn't noticed.
Talking about it wastes me.

Pain is methodical, don't make me prove it.
You'll be an animal inside a week.
Unleash the predator, canny, resigned.
Make sure he hasn't had his cake.

Let loose the ghosts in a fight to the life.
Nobody bothers to quote me.
Sleep might as well save me now.
What is left for me to glean?

IX.

It occurs there is still to reveal the muses
that transcribe the noises of me thinking,
who beat me to things I wanted to say,
till it hurts like a jilting to read, and reread.

More jaded than even an idol could notice,
researching every tiny sensation,
sometimes I just flail the air.
People wonder whether I'm caught in a web.

A roll is required to tick off the names
of each of the aspects for blood, or for good,
those gone and who remain, some only to do as they please.
They quote Shakespeare and it isn't even him.

My demands for perfection distract from TV.
All change can be accomplished by remote.
These are my thoughts: I will not remember later
what they expect in return.

It’s always a sentiment they describe
in a process for which there must be a label.
They follow each shot with remorse.
What I am, they remind, is unsure.

Presence is the muse who says she is this very moment.
Every night I close the blinds she every morning opens.
I perform CPR but can never save her.
She dies in my arms, I can still taste her.

In accepting unsure I become afraid,
a logical sequence to core motivation.
Fear is knowledge pain exists.
Muses pop pricked by its surface.

Leave a residue that hates itself
with which fear glues its tooth back on.
Only me with your back might be worse than alone.
We were just having fun when the point became serious.

X.

I don't wait for Polyhymnia,
nor does her eloquence pervade me.
I try to photograph the lightning but only get the rain.
Tap grape and lowly hop and bean and weed.

I wrote first of wolves and sheep,
how I forget which one I am.
How every hour spent alone further tests resolve to fail.
How Plan B is already compromised.

But what if she helps me find an expression?
What if she's a vivacious nychthemeral synesthete
who proves it serendipitous my mom misspelled my name.
Invite her purely into mind to touch decay.

Stare back into my line, luminescing.
Up the heat to incandescing.
An intensity from the wielder of the pen,
weighing the night's creativity against a 6 AM alarm.

A muse of sorts, the flaky Xena emails a jpeg,
spelling atrocious for her position.
Nude pixie in hibiscus, I suppose,
plenty to intrigue a verse.

I convey my respects to the aura she breeds,
admire her attachments,
one topless, another in a corset,
for my signature, loaded compliments:

I'll bet you've stirred the glands of many with those.
A muse if ever I dared exchange.
The Likeness might make a difference now, should anyone believe.
A red stroke on the list of things.

Ah, beautiful Xena, you should have been a starlet.
You're too illiterate to be a teacher.
Come across, my love, I'm not quite drunk yet,
and no longer care how rainbows work.

XI.

Once, I knew where God lived.
I could see from Vista Del Mar at sunset, looking north.
Man I was humble then.
Falling seemed like flying to the end.

There's a time to crave the heat,
to dull the ache, conclude the shine.
Honey sparkles to be like I do.
But what I wouldn't give to move myself again.

We haven't defined a feeling yet, but isn't it motion?
Doesn't it crave?
Small talk of dying, jump in the back,
on another day when, damn, I'm hapless.

Muses of beauty, know who you are.
Tell me again of the dogwoods splashing.
I doubt the names of flowers, and trees,
because everyone should understand the source of their beliefs.

No point in having a light if you don't turn it on.
Muses arise in a longing to describe
pure conjecture as skewed in a straightforward way.
I picture their faces and imagine what I'd say if I were me.

Contrast Faith, with standards so vicious,
what point in trying to meet?
Even orgasm would bleed.
Her breeze burns too. Otherwise, I'd get off easy.

Muses, get dressed, it's time to come home.
Who let you get laid more than I do?
If I think with my dick then blow my mind.
Catholic school did all our asses in.

Rilke, Berryman, what *shall* we do?
When the Likeness reveals his inner self,
symbolic will prove the disguise.
May he be a rubber offer on us all.

XII.

Can't somebody take a cue and find me?
Perhaps I've overly tainted the clues.
Scattered the crumbs till they're eaten by birds.
None can configure my camouflage face.

I see so far ahead at chess I resign after white's first move.
There's only one best choice at any time.
I spoke these words eight seconds ago
but they are just reaching you now.

All specific knowledge is a form of language,
so speak convinced the grass is green and back away.
My greatest fear is to be alive and not think these things.
Who could write this and not desire more?

I'll have ferment all day in my head to hang over,
meditate the process of decay,
give the globe a spin and let it roll me.
I stepped on a hummingbird. This is not a sign of anything.

Quit calling, you sellers of wanton surprises,
for I am a bible relentless of rain.
Sing me the beggars of proverbs, with sons
named after battlefields and daughters after whores.

There becomes a dank replacement
for the undercurrent afterglow.
I request you do not read this, please,
you have no right, I do not believe.

There's this uncertainty I must address
before crashing at usually two or so.
Among my defenses, a mirror, a glare.
No one predicts my future. No one.

I can't do anything I promised.
Refer to my tune, oblique, indecent.
On the string to the door beneath your feet,
my fingers, oops, too late.

XIII.

Muses, why do you wail? Cease.
These, too, will all be lies.
It isn't even dusk,
and you can't hide what you've done to yourself.

You'd better take a rest with your glow for a turn.
Survive, for his sake, you bubble in a church.
Where you wonder to the table at your wares.
When your deity is Murgatroyd you can't expect results.

Did you get your worth in these paltry sayings,
be-shaken in their rhythms and their robes?
A din could be amused with less.
You've become anemic, or something, in your soul.

I'm having too much fun for this to last.
Death won't let anyone just play with words.
It's given me creditors to keep.
I look through only one eye at a time.

Refuse to occur in this form to anyone else.
Can't even call the visions dreams, just
images of disconnections, missing when it's time to read.
Party of one, your knife is ready.

And they are searching, always searching.
Wouldn't dreams find things once in a while?
O'Hara, Crane, I see those muses on your faces
cast shadows on the moon during eclipse, proving earth round.

Let us instill our brains in one another.
Recap in frivolous delight the morning while we await
the darkest return of our pieces
to surface these feelings of needles with meat.

Yes! Let us juice them till we scream,
while these very idols quake my hands by day.
I have spoken, make it so, in silence.
How soon can a statue replace the Likeness?

XIV.

Punch is what we're really after.
A cry from the dark for a lull
in the interim sobriety.
Thanks to earplugs I fear neither lawyer nor poet.

Hope had her favorite medieval king:
Eric the Unforgettable.
She sought the most powerful man in the world as a genuine goal.
Either saw a rat gnaw a bone into a flute or is a liar.

Hope looked you up much as she's going to.
Accustomed to being right,
she wonders why she tells you anything.
Vision, ah, how the lions envy.

Can you forgive appearance here, fossilized like the first crow?
Overlook me like a vista!
Nail me to a tune, you amber delay.
Whisper Dysnomia, moon of Eris.

Once we were reasonable, and she the edgier sarsen stone.
A finger known for its curse.
I vow to free myself like Hope each morning,
by night to see the idol-slayer flee.

Don't disregard how muses abuse me.
Write me from the old world, so I can whiff your DNA.
I always wish from across the waves
but my wishes never break the orbit of my greed.

Hope says it's rough being everyone's friend.
With no designs on being saved,
I store my brain in the rest of humanity.
Not one to be brave for, merely wish me a paved way.

That's a punch to the bone, not the heart, I believe.
For the next few hours I'll drink to myself.
Hope is altar to my neediness,
so I look forward to her failure.

XV.

I, as you know, am a third of reality.
The Likeness would cut out his brain for a sequel.
He adores himself about you.
Of course he's going to be alone.

His knack is underestimation.
The story of how he came to be here
leads to the end of this sentence then is gone.
With what shall I replace its hunger?

The sound I make a search, and know,
in the numbness, you'll try not to do to your son
what your father did to you, and never die.
I still toast his photograph.

I love you, publish my poetry.
No, I'm not going anywhere, and yes, this is the poetry.
The Likeness so simplifies silence it makes dogs masturbate.
He's a windowless room with a bucket of light to no avail

who'd mail-order Styrofoam to see how it's wrapped for shipping.
Truth needn't even go in one ear.
In fact, there's something wrong with you for listening.
If God can make the stupid smart, keep praying.

Earth is the dirt of the sun
and its grains distilled make a man forget
his hymn contains the recipe for beer.
Then does he want to plant a crop!

Raze every tree till there's barley to go around!
If he could take a drink and stop he'd be all right,
but craves sufficient distance to see sunrise every 45 minutes.
No need to have sharp teeth when you die.

Hunters, the civilized kill.
Longing for connection,
the drunken Likeness splurges on cornflakes.
And Lord, how he can't stand milk.

Smoke & Stone Grant an Interview

Part One

When dealing in haze,
does variety matter?

It's most assuredly all the difference.
The Stone keeps secrets the crowd holds dear.
Stone and I are one, changing form,
destination and anchor, interconnected.

A simple problem of timing,
my equation? Never mind.
Let's just say I abide my own rule.

Shall light creep in
from under the cracks?

Yes, perhaps, but not while I'm here.
Such feats are accomplished while I'm still asleep –
if lies paid a wage though we'd all be high.

Where do the hours go to hide?

The sun elicits, the moon corrupts,
endlessly churning, remaining untouched,
but only this much can I share:

Between thinking and sensation
neither claims to be at the wheel.
If you see them together pretend not to notice.
At least that's what they'd have me believe.

Part Two

This, the Stone told me to ask:
Of giver and taker, which is which?

Now, at last, we get down to it.
I think I hear a kind of calling,
in the distance, growing stronger.
I can fly where none remember,
in an hour, you'll be dust again.

I cursed that wretch, the wind,
but will not drag it down forever offended.
Trust in martyrs or betrayers, what do I care?
Once, maybe so, but no longer.
I'm not in charge of how things work out.

Flip backward an instant to find out what happened,
call it religion, reactions prescribed.

Build your church out of blood, if you will.
At best it can make you a decent write-off.

Where then, shall the truth lie?

The truth is just this: I say what is right!
Sometimes, around me, people get hurt.
Accept the knife with sincerest apology.
The arrow flew straight,
it's the earth that curved.

I sway the course of events,
but only temporarily.

(Says Smoke to Stone:
We blame each other).

Part Three

Then what of the flame,
to which you aspire?

Ha! A primitive fool, the fire.
Possessing no sort of self control,
it expends its resources till I'm left alone.
As it is, I dabble in atmosphere,
and what an ash the sun's gonna make.

Were it left up to you
who could have been saved?

To be clear, as a vapor, I'm not a saint.
I've laid a lot of lines to waste.
Planted acquaintances like seeds
as if the bone grew into flesh
and breath could return to claim it.

But fire, as you know, is tainted,
and wind my immortal enemy.
The home they built me has been condemned.
The rule to face is dissipation.
Few would share their meat with flies.

According to Stone,
sanity falls but never rises –

(Rebukes the Smoke with hammer and chisel:
Who can say?)

Part Four

If the breeze turns the page
is it out of my hands?
I must have forgotten to mention the ghosts!
No wonder; I've stolen more than my share.

They enter on any hollow sound
and lay their eggs at the back of the mouth.
Evil maggots breed on the brain.
If you fear they're hatching, cover your ears.

When they come out of nowhere, I give them a name.
Labeled, they answer to me thereafter.
It requires a feeling for time elapsing.
A leak in the energy somewhere.

I raced jealous gods here and hungry demons,
disguised as sacramental wine.
In provocative tones begged, T*ake a hold.*
I've come on my own, no spirits to guide me.

I show them their rooms without windows, or walls,
where only the shapeless can enter.
Just disregard other forms of light,
we'll spin beyond gravity awhile.

I've already slept with you often in dreams,
brought lust and desire enough for one night.
Imagine it though! Eternally high!
Free to ring any bells you like.

I'll inscribe your name someplace wherein it may linger,
quoted verbatim, for others to see.
Take my word, this is no mere belief,
they'll utter it deep inside their being,

and for that single moment, it will seem real,
as if you've come back to life in their eyes.
(Then he twisted, as if to wrest
the head from the poem so it couldn't be cited).

Part Five

Stone, of course, strongly disagrees.
She shows me her infamous heart collection.

Many, she confides, are artifacts.
Sculptors, warriors, astrologers, kings,

some of whom you may have heard.
But it mostly consists of those you won't.

Poor men, beggars, poets and thieves.
Idolaters who sold their teeth to fairies.

The most gallant knight here couldn't conquer a worm.
You know, the earth is partly stone,

and you, you arose from it too,
a hole ago in my eternity.

Standing here looking out over the fields,
smoke is quiet, gone from view,

but all that has life, according to stone,
to her, eventually, will return.

So although mere sayings can never dissuade,
from those here engraved I'm inclined to believe,

Stone is a prophet, Smoke, a liar.

Chess

I want to be with those who know secret things or else alone.

RILKE

The Game Begins

I am not as good at chess as I dream. More a poet at it.
But the pre-beginning creates itself right after the beginning.
It's ironic, because the beginning has to happen first,
the former being timeless.

And it's no judgment, to call the pre-beginning timeless.
It simply follows its own rules. Go back to when we first
agreed to play. "Let's set up the board," we said,
and moved the pieces into place, part of the game.

We can't just start with everyone scattered.
Positions must be occupied. Otherwise, when can we say
the game began? A few weeks ago when we both discovered
we knew the rules and said we should get together?

Of course not. The game began after the pieces were set.
That way we agree upon an official beginning.
And if the beginning is first, the pre-beginning is zeroth,
because it came before the first.

The Board

What happens to one cell affects the whole.
The body affects the place in which it dwells,
and the place affects the earth, the stars, and so on,
back to the equivalent of before the game began.

Here is law in action:
What happens above happens below.
When I say whole, I mean everything,
evolved together with its place.

On the board position is specific.
Each piece enforces to its degree. No two on the same square.
And the power of any piece is more than ability
to take another out of play. All have that.

A Pawn can regard the Queen and mate the King.
The key is to get in and out of the way.
To take up space.
Divert.

The King

A king is hardly better than a pawn,
except it can backpedal, step aside.
Stands a head taller, in its crown,
to be checked, but never taken.

Taken means removed from the board.
Generally, for the rest of the game.
That is to say, for life.
No starting over to the pieces,

with one exception:
A pawn that fights
to the very last row promotes to any piece it pleases.
Except another king.

The Pawn

A pawn can never step back,
nor to the side,
leaving no place from grid eight to go.
It just stands there looking over the edge.

Of course it is transformed by that.
Can be rook if it wants to, bishop, or knight.
Maybe even another pawn,
back at the beginning of life.

And it wouldn't be stupid, to be itself again.
For a new pawn to pop up where it began
and change the whole direction of the contest.
So sacrifice a piece to win, because mate is the object.

The king must always stand.
If he lies down the kingdom is taken.
The question is whether he can keep
another in its square.

If he cannot move,
he's like a pawn.
And then what queen would have him?
He can't even turn into anything.

The Queen

She can move in any direction,
but can't break the boundaries of the grid.
None can.
No leaving the field.

And even though the board is preset at the beginning,
it morphs into countless situations.
I cannot say for certain if it's finite,
though the plane itself has edges.

But if the big bang is an explosion still expanding,
those most ancient, outermost parts lead
to John describing this, then continue
on ever more molecular levels of space inside and out him.

So no matter how random the point
something begins from seems to be,
there becomes, that moment and thereafter, the pre-
beginning,
like a chessboard set for the very first move.

It makes no difference that the start is arranged,
that it's "set up,"
that there's a beginning and an end.
That life lasts as long as the game continues.

To measure time we pick a random moment to begin.
Light moves.
There is no point in being light if you don't.
The dark it moves into reveals itself.

"The flesh is sad, alas, and I have read all the books."

Stéphane Mallarmé

Descended of Thieves

Part One

After just a few hours, I'm by myself.
The one who made me called it a day.
I've forgotten the names of things,
and yet, am wondering what to wear.

Was it yesterday I went mad?
It's the smell of knowledge beckoning
from every fork, and bend.
That scent which marks my boundary.

Had it not flown here to breach me, well….
Hello! Is someone there to help?
Only dark responds:
I am.

Then I went back inside my head
and believed it must have been a dream,
not some lovesick, restless flight
where every sound I hear is music.

On my line, I reeled a hole that opened,
blurting out a butterfly.
When it established an orbit around me, I swatted.
Shot off my mouth like a star into night.

I woke to a loud knocking.
Opened the door – it was the wind.
Are you the clay, the dust, the ash?
I answer, 'that's what I fear.'

Then freeze, it says,
or I'll blow you away.

The fire is there to back him up.
They warn the tree to get ready –

we caught him with the sun in his eyes,
and the moth-wing slime of light on his hands

Part Two

They proclaim, just in case,
a Hell is required.
Nearly everyone volunteers,
my ancestors among them.

They tear down the gallows to stoke the flame.
In the form of a serpent, the judge arrives,
hung from the rafters like a rope.
He gets right into my face and hisses:

Isn't that a lump in your throat?
"No! I didn't do it! I just yanked the hook
and threw it back already dead. The depths
all carefully measured by the jawbone of an ass."

Why would you make up a word for mother?
By glow of cigarette they probe.
We caught you two together naked.
Would you like to explain to us what you were doing?

"Damn, I haven't a clue where she came from.
And she's not quite my species, notice the hair.
If I appear shaken, don't worry,
I'm sure it's only the sedation."

What of your mother, isn't she missing?
And your first wife too, what was her name?
You didn't think we knew about her.
Tell us, exactly, where you've been hiding.

I examine probabilities,
arrive at too many conclusions,
crave to tell a convincing lie.
"Define please, what you mean by *where*?

Is it in the entire scheme of things,
relative to my existence,
or particular location
on a map you had in mind?"

They murmur among themselves in agreement,
nod their heads in unison:
Definitely good and evil –
Guilty as charged.

Part Three

Either the bench or the chair then suggested:
Why don't we string him up by his teeth?
Then, to the fire, whispered
Isn't our little project complete?

"Wait! I wasn't anywhere that day, believe me!
It came to this, I didn't mean it.
It's all her fault – the woman did it!
She cheated when we broke the wishbone!"

Declared the rope, aware of a loophole:
Give us your version of where you came from.
"My father is the unbearable sun.
My mother is the earth that raised me.

I never had any formative years.
Only hours ago, I woke with a name,"
(Muttered the gavel to the sword
I told you he'd be suspicious....

The broom in the corner said
Please, carry on).
"My first wife sold herself to night,
who made her a constellation.

I killed my brother for his skin.
It was dark, and I was cold.
I used the foot of a mountain to beat him,
then made shoes, and an overcoat.

Other elements were jealous.
The water despised my air-breathing form,
the fire, of course, obsessed by bone.
Come to think of it, I'm an orphan,

I've always been alone."

Part Four

The others got all the music.
This is my power –Words.
My first wife never understood.
She gave me a grunt when it was small.

I brought it up.
Was I supposed to let it die?
It became a giant tongue
that licked my face and washed my back.

It's the tongue that eventually got her.
I could not only give names, but call them.
Big ones, that knew what to break.
I controlled it, at first.

They used to come running
whenever I summoned. But after a while
they tired of it. Transformed
into wine and took everything over –

then told me I was going to die.
Can you imagine? Me! Their maker!
My philosophy now: trust no one.
Keep that will stashed out of sight,

right beside the family jewels,
or in the frame, behind a photograph.
Then if anyone inquires, tell them
that's the one of me, my finger

steady on the trigger,
hoping for nothing to soon set it off.
I make a living on the six,
if the price isn't years, it's nothin'.

I practice repeating over and over,
What are you lookin' at, chump?
Hey, I ain't no poet, jack,
millions are doomed to be me, and why?

I swear it was the woman told me
the infinite moon was mine.
Can you blame me for what I believe?
Yes, if we believe we can.

Part Five

The judge insists:
Enough of this drivel.
We warned you this morning,
the terms understood.

The woman couldn't possibly…
We created her later that afternoon.
Obviously, she couldn't have known.
Now the curse is on, so beat it.

It all worked out pretty much as it should,
get lost, and don't come back alive.
Assemble enough thieves,
and there'll be nothing they can't accomplish.

But inasmuch as you're a gambler,
I'll give you a chance to go for broke –
Your fantasies for your fears?
Throw down your wobbling Jello of flesh

and bet it all to succumb as before
to addiction, your surest wager.
Meanwhile, a small orange fish
oblivious to evaporation blows rings

throughout a bowl it thinks the ocean,
soon to wriggle in a puddle
against a suffocation all its own.
How ignorant.

Mass

Every action of nature is perfect.
Every action of *nature* is perfect.
Every action of nature is *perfect*.

This has been a recitation of the law.
You may go now.

Photo: Hélène Cardona

JOHN M. FITZGERALD is a poet, writer, editor and attorney for the disabled in Los Angeles. A dual citizen of the United States and Ireland, he attended the University of West Los Angeles School of Law, where he was editor of the Law Review. *The Mind* was published by Salmon Poetry in 2011. His first book, *Spring Water,* was a Turning Point Books prize selection in 2005. *Telling Time by the Shadows* was released in April 2008 by Turning Point Books. As yet unpublished works include Primate, a novel and screenplay, the non-fiction *The People of the Net*. He has contributed to the anthologies *Poetry: Reading it, Writing it, Publishing it* (Salmon Poetry), *Dogs Singing: A Tribute Anthology* (Salmon Poetry), and *From the Four-Chambered Heart: In Tribute to Anais Nin* (Sybaritic Press) as well as to many literary magazines, notably *The Warwick Review, Barnwood Mag, Askew Poetry Journal, Spillway*, and *Lit Bridge*.